AFTER PARK ROAD

THE NEXT CHAPTER

ANDREW HOPKINS

Copyright © 2021 by Andrew Hopkins

Published by DS Productions

All rights reserved. No part of this publication may be reproduced, distributed, or transmitted in any form or by any means, including photocopying, recording, or other electronic or mechanical methods, without the prior written permission of the publisher, except in the case of brief quotations embodied in critical reviews and certain other noncommercial uses permitted by copyright law.

ISBN: 9798513571094

❦ Created with Vellum

It takes great courage to write a book. It takes strength to put your soul into something that means a lot to you personally. I would like to dedicate this book to my children – Pixxie, Orla, and Killian. You show me each day how important it is to be honest and true to yourself. You make me smile 24/7 and keep me going through the doubts I have in myself.
Also to Becci for putting up with me and believing in me. And let's not forget putting up with the spooky happenings that occur at home when I write. Thank you!

The path circled around, and before I realised it, the background noise of the road and the busy pub had disappeared. I turned a corner and there was a low bridge in front of me. It seemed to emanate darkness. I looked through the bridge to the other side and it seemed to distort and wave in the wind. I felt sick, and I remember the shivers creeping up my spine as a voice inside me told me to go back. I took a step closer and the sickening feeling intensified, and the shadows of the surrounding trees seemed to encircle me and push me forward. The warmth from the sun had slithered away.

I was afraid of this place, frightened away by something so simple as a bridge. Yet, I remember the excitement, too. My heart seemed to welcome the feeling of something out of the ordinary, and I felt a smile grow on my face. Looking back, this was probably the same kind of smile you see in the movies before the bad guy commits some major atrocity. I must have looked crazy.

I was under the bridge and the walls pulsed with their own life-force. I heard whispering all around me—different voices, singing voices and loud bossy voices. These didn't stop me; they enchanted me and drew me in more. I was not scared in the way I thought I would be. It felt surreal, like these voices were singing for me.

The underside of the bridge that formed the tunnel I was under was not a long one. In reality, it would take less than five seconds to walk through, but I seemed to be trudging through quicksand. I turned slowly to look at the details of the bridge. The bricks were covered in moss and sludge, similar to the inside of a giant's mouth, I thought. It smelt how I could imagine that would, too. Vandalism on the walls told stories of past loves and crude drawings of oversized manhoods. Burn marks created soot patterns on the roof like deformed bats and ghouls.

My feet crunched on broken glass; the remains of a beer bottle were scattered on the uneven ground. I felt as though I were in a trance. My head was filling up with the whispering voices and my eyes were captivated by the patterns on the bricks. My body was

1

THE RUINS

The area around Coalville in Leicestershire, England is not short on ghost stories. There is a tale of a spectral black cat who stalked around the woods, there are hotspots around the rocks, and even a tale of a hooded spirit who looks like the Grim Reaper. However, this night my destination was the haunted ruins forty-five minutes from home. It was a nice evening, the sun was still warming the world at seven p.m., and it was just starting to set by the time I got to the carpark to the wooded walk that led to the ruins.

The carpark was quite busy. It is next to a pub and restaurant and so it was the perfect night for people to be out for a beer and some food. The people in the beer garden didn't even pay attention to me wandering up and heading straight for the pass, and why would they? The first part of my journey this night was quite beautiful. The trees were huge and green, the sunlight casting orange and gold beauty to the leaves. The birds sang their early evening song and in my heart I felt relaxed and free, walking through the soft grass. I looked around at the closely knit trees and thought it would be best if I had remembered a torch for when it got dark, but being me, I had hurried without thinking.

Foreword

something more. My mind cast over to memories of my childhood, of the old lady I met in my room who is as vivid a memory in my mind today as it was back then. I remember the feeling of dread I felt in the terrors I encountered in my old house, but I also remember the feeling of being alive, of fighting for my life... and I missed it.

I remember sitting on my bed, staring out of the open window, the warmth of the summer evening drifting in, and thinking *I need more!* I was growing up, and I believed that even in the six months that had passed since we left Park Road, my senses were seeming to get weaker and close down. I had learnt a great deal about myself at Park Road, and I knew if I needed something done, or if I wanted to achieve something, then I must go looking for it.

I had no idea how I would evolve or how I would grow spiritually, but I took a chance and threw myself in the deep end once again. It was a beautiful summer evening, and I was bored and feeling like a cat in a bag, not a great mixture for a young man around eighteen years old looking for answers. I got dressed, grabbed a jacket and went out for a walk...

FOREWORD

It is said that our life experiences change us. They mould us into the person we are to become. Through our troubles, through our victories, we become who we are because we are shaped by our experiences. I am Andy, and I see ghosts. Through living my life within the walls of a most haunted house in Coalville, Leicestershire, England, the house on Park Road thrust me into the world of the paranormal, and I could not switch it off anymore.

It had been six months since I left Park Road for the new house only twenty minutes away. This new house seemed hollow; it seemed empty and almost dead. The floors didn't creak, the walls were freshly painted, and the lighting was fancy. When you walked into this house on Margaret Street, you could see through the house to the end of the kitchen. There were no eyes staring and no fear at all.

I was not wishing for spirits appearing out of the walls, and I was not hoping to be disturbed and in need of spiritual protection as I was in the old, foreboding house, but this one seemed to be lacking that spark that my spiritual side needed. I found myself feeling drained and feeling lost in this soulless house. I didn't want to give up on this path; my mind had been opened and my sight was searching for being consumed by this energy. I had no idea what was happening, and I didn't care.

One voice sounded out loudly above the rest, and I was snapped out of my trance. "Andy, leave!" It was a lady's voice and she spoke with an authority that I could not ignore. A flash of a dark green uniform spilled across my vision and vanished. I was standing with my feet planted in the middle of the tunnel as the feeling of urgency filled my head and I smelt smoke. I ran forward, and within a second I was through the tunnel and the light from the setting sun hit me like warm water. My chest was gasping as though I had run a marathon, and I bent over to rest on the balls of my feet, catching my breath. The tunnel seemed layered in mist, dark and clinging to the ground. I looked up to the face of the bridge where the graffiti read NO ESCAPE! I was surrounded by images of crying faces.

That's new! I thought to myself. I had never experienced anything so vivid in a public place, and that voice, that lady's voice seemed stronger than I had expected, too. I brushed myself off and turned to face the stone path in front of me. Trees were on both sides of the path and the sky was turning a beautiful pinky-blue above me. I felt calm again, and I also felt quite exhilarated by the experience I just had. It was as though my spiritual senses were stretching and shaking off the dust.

I was ready to set off. I took one look at the bridge and started to walk the path. The stones were crunching beneath my feet and the dust rose slightly, caking my shoes in grey dust, but apart from that things were okay. I stopped to get a stone out of my shoe to hear the crunching of rocks behind me. There was a man with a dog behind me about one hundred yards away. He was moving slowly, looking at me. The feeling of his stare intensified. He was far away but I felt his stare. His grey-checked flat cap cast a shadow over his brow and gave the impression of anger as he trudged closer to me. His dog was a sheepdog with long black and white fur that moved in the warm breeze. It was panting and pulling the old man forward, but the old man didn't seem to be struggling. He got closer to me and his eyes continued to glare, burning into me. I noticed his grey trousers looked scuffed around the knees and there was the sign of blood seeping through.

Sometimes we can see people and they immediately give us the creeps. Our bodies tell us to run, and we should not ignore this feeling; however, I was stupid. I stayed braced by the side of the path as this man and his dog got closer and closer. I could hear the dog's panting breath, but the man made no sound but the crunching of the gravel underfoot. He came level with me and his head turned to look at me. His neck made this horrible sound, like creaking wood, clicking bone on bone, and it made me feel sick in the pit of my stomach. I smiled and asked if he was okay. I saw the state his knees seemed to be in and I thought he may need help, but he simply ignored me, walked past, and disappeared around the corner ahead of me.

I was curious about this man. I felt as though there was something off about him. I cannot say he was a ghost, but I do know that my senses were telling me this encounter was not just as simple as an elderly dog walker, passing by me. I did hurry after him as he turned the corner, but he was gone without a trace.

This next part of the walk to the ruins started with large pillars that hold up an old waterway. I had strange feelings about this place. Although this structure dwarfed me, I felt like it was Everest; it made me feel small and nervous. I could hear the water above, swishing and crashing over the side, and it made my eyes water. *Why am I crying?* I felt my emotions start to overtake me and I felt sad and scared. There was no water spilling from above me and the wind was not nearly strong enough this evening to make the water fierce.

I needed answers to whether the sounds were real and not in my head. Getting up to the waterway required a climb through the brush and trees up a steep incline. Not the best thing to do in shorts, I must say. As I climbed, my emotions calmed down but the sound of the water rushing past was louder than ever. The brush was thick and spiky. My legs were getting scratched up, and more than once, a tree hit me in the face like a comic sketch from *Tom and Jerry*.

However, I persevered and made it to the top. I was shocked by what I saw. There was no water, just mud and overgrown grass that had taken hold of this old structure. The sound of water had stopped and had been replaced by the sound of my thumping heart from my climb. I was dumbstruck as to how clearly I had heard this water and yet there was no sign of it. The ground on this structure was dry.

After sitting for five minutes, contemplating what had happened, I decided it was time to carry on. Half of me was not sure I should after the experiences so far, but brave explorer and ghostbuster Andy Hopkins was in charge right now. I half-climbed and half-fell down the bushy embankment to the ground below to continue onwards. This path was much darker, and not just because the sun was setting. The bushes and the trees on each side come closer and cut into the path as the path turned from gravel to dirt.

The smell was fresh and sweet in the summer breeze, but my body was getting colder the farther I walked into this new part of my adventure. At a point halfway through the woods, there is a slight veering off point where you can go into the bush or continue to the ruins. I stood captivated by the route through the woods. There was a formation in the trees in the distance that looked like a hooded figure. I felt this force from within me urging me not to go down that path, and this time I listened and opted for the dirt path to the ruins.

I opened the gate and heard shouting. "Oi!" this voice called. There was no one there, just the dying echo of this shout. I stopped waiting for the source of this shout to show themselves. I knew I was not supposed to be along this walk after sunset, so I assumed I was going to be told off by some ranger or caretaker, but no one appeared, so I continued.

It always amazes me how hundreds of years ago people could build such amazing structures with little technology compared to today. Even those ruins seemed to be a massive feat of architecture. The ruins used to be a women's priory, and it had the legend attached to it of the grey lady, a spirit seen wandering around the ruins and along the road that ran to the side of the site. The grounds felt peaceful. The setting sun made the shadows of the bigger structures stretch out for what seemed like forever. The old stones were piled with such precision that this would have been such a sight when it was whole and newly built.

I didn't feel fear at all around this area, even with the darkening sky. I wandered around the walls and through the archways of this beautiful place, and I was in awe of it. I could hear the noise of footsteps that, at this point, I thought was in my mind, as nothing like that would be able to be heard on the grassy ground. There was the occasional car speeding by along the distant road but other than that, it was lovely. I sat down on a grass verge overlooking what would have been the communal area of the priory and just watched. There was a feeling of busyness. I felt as though I was in the way and like I shouldn't be sitting there. It was not oppressive, but I felt the grounds of this place, meant predominantly for women, was not happy with a young guy just sitting and watching.

I heard a whistle that startled me, and as I turned to look in the direction from where it came, I saw the glimpse of a shape that went behind a tall chimney structure. I got up and ran in that direction only to find nothing at all. This felt different than the peaceful feeling from before. I felt baited, drawn there for a purpose. The whistle happened again. This time it felt as though it came from the walls towards the far end of the ruins. I knew it felt wrong, but I went towards the source of the sound. Once again there was nothing there, but the temperature was dropping rapidly and the sky had switched from beautiful amazement filled with stars to nightmarishly dark. Although the stars above were bright, they did very little to illuminate my surroundings. The occasional headlights from passing cars provided all the light I had, but as the car lights hit the ruins, it made shadows dance around me like a dance of doom. It was time to leave, but the path out of the ruins seemed dangerous. The woods seemed to grow teeth like a ravenous monster seeking fresh meat. I edged towards the path, daring not to look up from my feet and the dark, muddy path.

Keep your eyes down. It'll be fine! I started humming songs in my head, trying to keep my mind calm. *Head down and hurry. It'll be fine...* Starting to sing a second song, my footfall fell to the same beat as an *Iron Maiden* tune that was now being blasted out as loud as possible to drown out the noises of the night. One lesson I learnt from this experience was never enter a potentially haunted location without a torch, but in that moment, I didn't want anything to illuminate what I felt was watching me.

I went slightly off track and lost my way. I reached a metal gate that led to another field. I stopped my singing and looked up. I could see the road and I could see the landscape of the field. There were silhouettes of a group of people in the middle of the field. I felt them looking my way just before I heard them shout to me. Logically, it is not the kind of thing you expect to see in a field in the middle of the night, but I was thankful to see anyone at that point who may be able to walk back to civilisation with me.

My breathing started to slow as relief sunk in. I shouted back to them and waved my arms to signal I was there—like a damsel in distress, I am sure. They started walking towards me, three of them. They walked next to one another in line, a perfect formation as the solid shadows of these people stood out from the dark. They walked closer and then something struck me about them. They were sinking into the ground and soon they were legless, then just their shoulders and heads, then nothing...

They should have reached my shaking form, but instead, they vanished into the earth. *Oh!* I went cold. My eyes couldn't look away from where I had seen these figures. Speechless and shaking with fear, I stood rooted to the spot.

I don't know how long I was there. My ears were ringing, and I had no idea what I was going to do. A sound from behind me shook me awake but there was nothing there. I set back off, marginally knowing where I was going. I was heading to where the pathway forked off. If I kept on going straight, I would reach the waterway, then all I needed to do was turn right and head for the tunnel and I was home free. This thought made me quicken my pace.

Breathlessly, I passed the fork, nearly tripping over the overgrown shrubbery. Then, I slowed. A sudden breeze blew down my neck and I stopped. *Don't look round!* It happened so suddenly; the hooded figure was in my face; featureless and eternal was the darkness of its form. It met my height exactly as I stared into the pitch-black void. I felt energy from this thing holding me. Motionless and voiceless, I was held in its embrace.

The edges of this entity faded and blended into the edges of the real world, and the sound it made as it held me in its force was like a gale force wind. It stood before me, swaying slightly. Its cloak seemed liquid as it swayed, encompassing its inner darkness where the body should be. It froze my bones and threatened to take my last breath. As suddenly as the thing appeared, it rushed away and down the fork in the road, and I felt my body drop to the ground. I heard this creature's stormy sound die down as I got to my knees.

My fight or flight reflex kicked in and I ran. I felt the nettles and the overgrown brush whipping at my legs as I reached the waterway and the towering pillars. I did not stop to see if any other ghostly thing wanted to say hello. I turned right and started to run towards the tunnel bridge. I heard dogs barking in the distance, and I hoped there was nothing chasing me. I skidded to a stop at the tunnel. I could see lights from the pub sparkling from a distance through the trees, and I ran through without a second thought, bursting out the other side like the cork in a champagne bottle. I was free and I had escaped.

It is funny how a place can change completely in a matter of a few steps. Upon exiting the tunnel and reaching the grassy path on the other side, the energy changed fully. It felt calm again. I had time to slow down my pace and my breathing as I walked back through the entrance to the carpark. It felt reassuring to hear the sound of laughter of those people in the pub surrounding me as I walked by, heading for the way home. In that moment I felt relief, of course, but I also looked back at the experience and thought *I just did that, and I survived!* Young and naïve I might have been, terrified I was, but I would not be stopped. I had felt more alive in the terror and had seen what many never would. This terrifying encounter only added to my longing to understand more and experience more.

I have returned to the ruins many times in my life, sometimes experiencing some horrendous things (more of those tales later). But I have never seen the hooded figure again. Then again, I have never been on that adventure alone again. I do feel that being alone in a place like this really does affect you differently.

2

BLACK EYES IN THE GRANGE

I found myself seeking out places to sit and think more and more and find places where I wanted to kind of get away from the world. Life was a confusing time for me when I was younger, not only the spiritual stuff but I could feel myself drifting away from people I hung around with, through no fault of their own. I felt quite like the odd one out. With my siblings off living their own lives and my parental figures all busy with their own lives, too, I sought out places to get lost in.

One place I found was a nature area and woodland walk close to the old colliery museum. It was literally at the end of the new road where we had moved after Park Road, so five minutes and you couldn't even hear the cars when you were in the woods.

I had developed a routine on my walks so as not to get caught in the same horror movie as I had before when visiting the ruins. I had my trusty torch, which was a silver *RAC* torch that could light up the moon with some decent batteries. I had spare batteries, and I had snacks and a flask of freshly brewed coffee. I also had gloves and spare socks because I had read having spare socks was important, like I was going to actually get lost in the woodlands around Coalville.

It was a Thursday in August so it was nice and warm, so off I went with my trusty backpack to venture out for some me time. I was supposed to be going on this little adventure with my friend, Michael, who I met at an arts class we had both attended. He had messaged me half an hour before the trip, cancelling to my annoyance, only saying that his girlfriend, Lucy, was having something of a meltdown and now wasn't talking to him. It annoyed me and we exchanged words about the short notice. Well, I actually had a go at him, which resulted in us falling out and me going solo.

It was early evening around six when I took my trip down the old gravel road past the football club. The air smelt like summer and the sky was blue with a few darker clouds that occasionally blocked out the sun. There was someone walking their dog who walked past me and smiled as I smiled at the dog. I felt calm and I could not wait to be beneath the trees and sit by the fishing lakes. My temper had started to calm down from my disagreement and annoyance with my friend, and the summer air was making me feel good. Once past the football club, I turned right through the turnstile and onto the winding road that leads to the fishing ponds. There was only one or two people fishing at this time, and as I walked past, they smiled and raised their hands soundlessly as not to scare away the fish. I had learnt the hard way to keep the noise down around fishermen, otherwise they got quite angry. I had been chased by one when I was younger and hanging around with my friend when we shouted, "Come on, fishies!" at the top of our voices.

The woods were peculiar here. In the daytime, they seemed to go on for miles. They were beautifully deep like something out of a fairytale. I remember times when we had come to hawking events here with the museum and had adventures during school holidays. I could almost relive these moments when I would walk by. I remember when I climbed the trees with my friend, Damian, and we fell into a bush of bristles and I cried my way back to my dad's house. In the daytime, there was a music to the woods. The wind would blow through the trees and the leaves would play the chords of adventure.

At night, however, the denseness of the woods was too thick and dark to see the light. The trunks of the trees would take on different forms—an ogre, a ghoul, or a witch. I never went into the woods at night down there. It was like crossing over into another world, and it frightened me. Not just because of what I could see and feel spiritually, but because I felt that there was something that could hurt me.

I had once been told a story by one of the colliery museum workers who had used to work in the pit at Snibston. His name was Paul, and he loved a good true story. He knew me because my mum worked cleaning in the museum as one of her many jobs she kept, so Paul always had time to tell me a tale. One day when I was walking to meet my mum from work, waiting in the café, he came up to me and started talking. "You like going down the nature park, don't you, Andy?" I had time for him. His friendly voice and approachable energy was always nice.

"I do, Paul. It's quiet and it's a nice place to think," I replied, not knowing exactly where this was going.

"Well, I don't know if you knew, but there used to be a house where those woods sit. It burnt to the ground one night. People said a witch lived in it." Paul's eyes were grey and old, lined with wrinkles that each told of stories like this. I listened intently; he could see that as he smiled back at me. "I don't know about witches, my lad, but I know something is down there." He was interrupted by a call put over the speakers for him to attend the front desk.

I had been to the grange countless times before during the day and seen nothing. I had been at night and seen nothing, too. Granted, I had never been in the woods at night.

It is funny what memories come back to you at times. Sometimes I find that memories are guided back by our spirit guides, sometimes to show spirit are near us, and sometimes as a warning.

I sat down on the grass facing the far fishing pond and lay back to look at the clouds. I love matching faces or images in clouds. It is like the sky takes away the negatives, and I had not realised how much negativity I felt about the altercation with my friend today. I could hear the wind through the trees, and I could hear the birds singing. The only traffic noise I could hear was one of the parked cars pulling off and taking one of the fishermen home. Then I felt someone watching me. This was nothing new, really, but I felt this feeling boring into my head. I turned around towards the treeline and saw the glimpse of a little girl. It was a split second and I told myself it could be my eyes playing tricks on me. I know I should have learnt by this time to trust myself, but it was true that sometimes we see faces in clouds that are just clouds, or shapes in trees that are just shapes in trees.

I went back to my cloudgazing. There was a whistle and a laugh as something pushed through the trees behind me. It felt playful, which didn't frighten me. I was brought back to a memory of the child spirit I encountered at Park Road. I could be that this child wasn't even a spirit at all; it could be that this girl could have been with a parent, taking a walk. I stared again towards the treeline but saw nothing. It was a little creepy because of the way this child was hiding, but still this felt harmless. It happened again, and this time as I turned around, I saw another figure walking behind the shadow of the trees. A sudden shiver hit me like a wave. I stood up and walked towards the treeline. It was not dark yet and I could still see the last remaining fisherman sitting patiently with his magazine, watching his line.

It felt cold under the trees, naturally. There was a gloomy green light as the low summer sun was starting to turn darker. There was no one that I could see here. I even called out to see if there was anyone walking who would answer me. But there was no one. It was gravely silent in the murky light.

The woods in this area are on different levels. The higher level leads on to a carpark that you access through the woods by going around the steep incline or clambering up the slope to reach the top area. It was slippery underfoot and quite muddy, but I wanted to hurry to check if there was anyone in the top carpark, so I opted to get to the higher ground quickly and went up the sharp slope. I twisted my ankle as I got caught on a vine and that sent a fresh stream of pain up my shin, too. This was seeming like the perfect time to think about calling time on my evening's adventure, but I was not ready to leave. *Don't be stubborn,* I told myself. I reached the top of the incline and walked the short distance to the carpark. The carpark was quite large but covered in moss and woodland waste, it looked overgrown like some lost world. The trees domed the top of the carpark and casted moving shadows from the tree puppeteer's shadow theatre above. No was there. As I walked towards the winding road and back down the easy way towards the fishing ponds, the last car pipped its horn at me and the fisherman waved his goodbye.

This was the point I should have left. Stubborn me decided I had not had enough me time. I shook off the experience of the little girl and the shadow I had seen through the trees and went back towards the ponds. The sky was starting to turn more orange and the warmth from the sun was dying away slowly. It felt calmer by the water and I felt the drama and the fights melt away. I took a slow walk around both ponds, watching as the insects slid and skated along the surface of the water. I knocked some of the flies away from my face and settled down on one of the benches by the water. I poured myself a coffee and blew away the steam before taking a drink. The hot coffee was beautiful. I took a further sip and smiled to myself. I relaxed into my sitting position and glanced around the scenery, my hands gripping the cup as the evening chill set in.

It was an hour or so that I was sitting on the bench, and it was calm with the leaves blowing in the trees. I was just enjoying nature and my coffee, but it was getting later and it was getting darker. I looked up towards the deepening blue sky, spotting the early evening stars. *I'll walk back soon,* I thought to myself. Drinking my last mouthful of coffee, I glanced towards the treeline over the water and saw the figure of a little girl and someone standing behind her in the dark of the trees. I spat my coffee out in shock. The little girl had dark eyes—no white was visible, just black. The dress was grey and crinkled with lace around the lower part. If it had not been roughed up and dirty, she would have looked like it was her best outfit. She looked about six years old with dark hair tied in plaited pigtails. Her face was blank, her expression empty of any emotion—she just stared with her bottomless black eyes fixed on me.

My eyes itched from the pollen but I couldn't blink. I looked up to the figure standing behind her. It was a female form in a dark blue dress, one pale hand resting on the little girl's shoulder. I couldn't make out details. I couldn't see fingers and I couldn't see a definite shape of her. There was a raggedy blue bonnet on her head but the shadow over her face made it impossible to see.

I reached into my bag for my torch and found the cold metal within my grip. My eyes never left the two spectres, but I knew where my bag was. Once my hand was on my torch, I pulled it out like a gunfighter in the Wild West. The beam of bright light hit the phantoms and they vanished. My breathing was fast and my heart was pumping. I moved the light around the treeline to see where they had gone. No sign of them anywhere.

"Andy, be careful!" the unknown female voice in my head rang out to me. I didn't know who she was yet, but I knew that she was trying to help me.

I brought the torchlight back to the ground beneath me and packed up my stuff, calmly and quickly. A branch snapped to my right-hand side and something flew out of the trees. My light was on the disturbance faster than I could say BOO! Nothing was there. *Just an animal!* I reassured myself. I turned around to pick up my bag and was greeted by the black-eyed girl standing before me. I screamed loudly enough to startle the birds in the trees and dropped my torch. The torchlight formed a round circle over where her legs should be, but the torchlight shone clear through her. The girl looked at the light, slowly and curiously gazing at it. My heart was beating, breaking out of my chest, and I was starting to hyperventilate. My face was cold and seemed wet as though there was dew settling on my skin. My fingers were stretched out as though subconsciously I was reaching out for something, anything to help me. She turned from the torch and back to me. Her head tilted as though she was studying me. Those eyes—never have I ever seen anything so black and so deep. It was as though these eyes were the window to pure nothingness. Her thin lips were pressed together on her pale face and her nose was small and flawless. She reached out and moved forward, farther into the torchlight, and vanished as I crouched down, preparing to feel the touch of this unknown spirit child.

I was crouched down with my arms over my head, breathing heavily. I felt like I was crouched that way for an age, awaiting the cold hands to touch my shoulder, but it didn't come. I looked up to see the circular beam of light rocking gently. The silver torch was rolling in the dirt. Quick as a flash, I grabbed the torch and shone it around the area. There was nothing to be seen; no one was in the treeline and no one on the path.

Fuck this! I ran around the lake to where the fishermen had parked earlier and where the start of the winding road was. My chest was burning but I couldn't stop. I had never seen anything like this child before. The memory of the pools of her black eyes sent a chill through me as I ran. The road was steep, and I had to slow down when I was level with the carpark. Something drew my attention to look to my right and to the abandoned carpark. *DON'T LOOK!* But I did look, and I saw the girl once again standing there at the entrance to the carpark. I set off running again but stopped as the figure I had seen earlier was standing in my way.

I wanted my instinct to kick in, I wanted my body to know what to do automatically, but it didn't. I stood panting and staring at this figure. I couldn't see her feet. She floated a few inches off the ground. The edges of her form blurred into the background. A low humming noise was being emitted by her. It could have been a tune or something, but it sounded far more eerie, and I had never placed the tune.

She was around ten meters in front of me. Stars were filling my vision as my body recovered from my run. The spectral lady started edging her way towards me, slowly gliding above the earth, menacingly promising to encompass me in her cold embrace.

Finally, my body took over and I ran, although I didn't run back to the ponds. I ran through the carpark, running past the little girl. This run was in slow motion, and as I passed the girl, I remember seeing her slowly turning her head as I went by her, those black, stony eyes shining in the torchlight. She blinked slowly as I ran by her and she vanished.

I fell down the embankment when I got beyond her. Nettles and thorns scratched and grazed my skin as I rolled down the hill and came to a stop at a fallen tree, knocking the wind out of me. Thankfully, I had kept hold of my torch, and after a moment or two I got up running. There was rustling all around me as my torch went this way and that way, searching for the stalking terrors of these phantoms. I could see the old picnic bench in the clearing, a nice place to sit during the day but now it looked like a giant crawling spider in my panicked head. There was a laugh, laughter of a little girl playing chase that was all too real. I turned around and saw her again. The light highlighted her perfectly, but she didn't disappear. The laughter emanated from around her, but her lips never parted. She stood there and the sound of more than one child laughing filled the air surrounding her. The spectral lady in blue came down the embankment, not stepping over the rocks or the thorns, but floating above them, through them.

The black-eyed girl held out her hand to me and tilted her head. Once again, the female voice in my head shouted, "RUN!" I didn't argue. I ran for the edge of the woods and did not look back. I was filled with a sickening feeling in my stomach. It felt as though I was being pulled back, but not me, more like my energy. My spirit was being pulled back. It was a strange feeling and one I have not encountered since that night.

I didn't stop because of this feeling, but I recall thinking the feeling was similar to how sailors were drawn to the rocks by a legendary Siren. This little girl had that kind of feeling, that power.

I reached the edge of the wood and the thin dirt track that forked left and right. If I went left, then I would reach the snaking road, but if I went right, I would reach a field that I could cut through and reach civilisation. The choice was made for me. I saw the spectral lady coming down from the winding road along the dirt path.

I turned and wrestled through the thinning overgrown path towards the metal foot crossing at the end of the trail. I slammed into the gate, my body smacking into the bar with the sound of a cymbal crash. I didn't dare take a second to glance behind me. I knew there was movement. I felt the cold black stare of the young girl watching me without even looking back. I pulled myself over the gate and fell into the muddy field headfirst. I clambered to my feet and ran forward a safe distance before looking back.

The two figures were standing there as they had been before—the young girl standing straight and proud in front of the deformed spectral lady. I walked backwards, staring at them. The girl looked up at the lady and the lady lowered her head to look at the girl. Soundlessly it looked as though they were exchanging thoughts. They both looked up and glanced at me again. The little girl raised her hand in a wave. Her thin lips raised into a small but sweet smile and those black eyes gleamed brightly. The lady faded away into the background and the black-eyed girl stepped backwards and was consumed by the trees.

I ran to the edge of the field towards the back of the houses along the street, snuck through a small entrance way and I was safe. I had reached civilisation and I was alive. My mind was racing with thoughts about what I had seen. It had scared me, but as usual, the buzz and the feeling of surviving another encounter with something unknown to the world at large made me feel glad and eager to learn more about these entities. I had only once heard of people reporting having seen children with black eyes and pale skin in woodland areas. It seemed to me this was just a different form of ghost, but it felt more like this child I encountered was more powerful and the lady who was accompanying her seemed to be helping her...

It was a strange occurrence, and it was one I was not sure I wanted to encounter again. I was tired by this time, and I took the five-minute walk through the square back home.

3

THE GIRL IN THE WARDROBE

I arrived home that night to find everyone asleep and the lights off. This didn't bother me, as I didn't find our home on Margaret Street nearly as scary as Park Road. I took off my muddy shoes and my jacket and flicked on the kettle. I was still wired from the events, and I had to speak to someone and tell them. I picked up the phone and was going to call my friend who had bailed on me. I decided against the phone call but sent him a message instead. Michael was always a little hard to get hold of. He didn't like mobile phones and was a bit of a conspiracy theorist, believing that mobile phones were being used to control us and that phones would take over our lives. Looking at this today, he was sort of right. But I sent him a quick message, saying, "Life is too short for falling out. Besides, you missed an epic spook fest tonight!"

He replied right away. "Sorry about earlier. Women! She still hasn't contacted me!" Then he called me and went on about saying he thought he had done something wrong again to annoy Lucy and force her to be silent with him. "I'm still trying to fix another imagined mess," he said in a tiresome way. "She freaked because I was not picking up while I was actually out..." He tried to laugh it off, but he was concerned. You could always tell with Michael when he was threatened about something by his tone of voice.

Michael was a friend I had known awhile since branching out and making friends. He was a believer in ghosts, but he wanted to see one. He and I got on well, even if we couldn't see one another as much as we wanted. He was working full time, and I was doing bits and pieces that kept me busy. But when we got together, we normally had a laugh.

To change the subject away from his personal dramas, I explained what I had seen down at the grange that night. He sounded shocked and gave me the "Are you kidding me?" line and asked for more details. We were on the phone for about an hour before I realised how tired I actually was, so I called time on the chat and said goodnight. We agreed to meet for coffee in the morning to catch up properly.

I got to my room and put a fresh cup of tea on my side table. My room in Margaret Street was smaller than at Park Road but it felt comfy. I had an oak wardrobe by the far side of the room and my metal frame bed by the window. I liked this position because I could see out onto the back garden, and when the window was open, it blew in a pleasant breeze.

There was an odd feeling in my room that night and although my head was tired, I could feel this draw. Someone was there. *You know what you're doing here, Andy!* I told myself. *Someone wants to talk to you. You got this.*

Conscious that the house was asleep, I kept things quiet. I lit a candle and turned out the light. I closed my eyes and I let myself relax. One, two, three—I counted each breath slowly and I asked my spirit guides to help me. I had no idea who they were at that time, but I knew I had them. I opened my eyes and stared at the wardrobe. It is the same feeling as when you see something you know you shouldn't. You try not to see it, but you cannot look away. That is the best way to describe how I feel when I know there is someone trying to talk to me.

"Is there anyone here who wants to talk to me?" I whispered in a low, calm voice. There was a creaking sound, and my wardrobe door slowly opened an inch or two. *This is tense...* I stared. The candlelight was flickering, and the room was silent. "I don't mean you any harm. I know you are there..." This was the first time I had felt something there or anywhere else that I knew was focused on wanting to communicate. It felt strong, determined, lonely. I closed my eyes and, in my head, I saw a girl. She wore pale blue jeans and a white t-shirt. She looked about twelve at most and she looked modern in my mind. It was not the "typical" ghost you see in a movie. This girl felt real and relatable. I opened my eyes and saw a glimpse of her standing by the wardrobe. It was as though the candlelight was highlighting one side of her, giving her pink skin a red and orange tint. I could see her blue eyes were crying. I could see the silvery traces of tears running down her cheeks and falling silently to the floor. She was slim and relatively tall for her age. I blinked and she faded.

Closing my eyes again, I saw her again. This time she was lying down in a hospital bed. I felt sick and had a pressure in my head that brought tears to my eyes. "Hannah," said a voice, silent and small. "Hannah," the voice said again. A shiver ran through my body like an electric current.

"What do you want, Hannah? I don't know who you are."

I heard a sob in response to my enquiry. It was a short sob that sounded as though she didn't want to cry. I felt so connected to this girl without even knowing who she was. I felt like I should know but I didn't. I wanted to help her... NO! I needed to help her! I could see the image she showed me of her in the hospital bed. She was connected to a lot of machinery and had a tube coming from her mouth. She looked in a bad way. Bandages were wrapped around her head and her face was swollen and blue with bruises. Her eyes were taped shut, and I could hear the beeping of the machines so loudly that I opened my eyes to make sure nothing in my room was going off. There was nothing but dancing candlelight in my room and the faint glimmer of the girl in the wardrobe.

After Park Road

I could see a lady beside her. She was holding the girl's lifeless hand while sobbing, makeup running down this lady's cheeks. She was dressed up and had her hair done nicely, and this seemed to make the image worse. The tiny voice spoke up again. "In the red box..." It felt important, even though she spoke in such a hushed voice.

"Who is the red box for, Hannah?" I asked calmly.

There was not really a response, but the energy changed. I felt anxious and jittery, which was a contrast to how I felt only moments previously. The peaceful feeling was vanishing from the room, but I kept my eyes closed, as I didn't want to lose the connection. In the vision I saw in my mind, an alarm started to sound loudly like the scream of some fearsome creature in pain. The lady was escorted out quickly and the vision ended, burnt away from my sight like paper in a flame. Blackness was now all I saw in my mind.

I felt a cold breeze on my face that made my face feel wet with the cold. I opened my eyes, expecting to see the dancing candlelight on my walls, but I was met by the girl from the wardrobe face to face with me. Her eyes were piercing, wide, and meeting mine square on. The tear tracks down her cheeks seemed to have left scars in her skin —red lines that looked sore and deep. I panicked and threw myself backwards in shock and hit my head on the windowsill. She shot back towards the wardrobe like a bull out of the gate and vanished with a slam of the wardrobe door.

What just happened?

I sat myself up, nursing the back of my head from the impact on the windowsill and shook my head while staring at the wardrobe. I didn't feel afraid. I knew this girl was not wanting to cause me harm, but her sudden appearance face to face with me made me jump. I hadn't expected that. I heard the hallway light click on and heard my stepdad, Malc, stumble across the landing and go into the bathroom next to my room. This made me glad that it was someone living making the noise outside. I waited for him to go back to his room before getting off my bed. I walked slowly to the wardrobe and opened the door. I didn't expect to see the spirit girl in there, but having checked, I was quite relieved. I returned to my bed. Blowing out the candle, I drifted off to sleep, forgetting all about my cup of tea.

The next day I woke up later than I had expected to. I heard the dogs barking downstairs and someone knocking at the door. I rushed out of bed to find the postman had left the dreaded red slip that means you missed the parcel. Not a great start to my day, but I didn't care. My mind was filled with questions of who this child spirit belonged to. I got myself ready and went to meet up with Michael at the local coffee shop. My friend looked tired, but he smiled and was happy to meet up, especially after the argument from the day before. He bought me a coffee as a way of apologising. To me, that is like someone buying me jewellery. It was good to catch up and he was asking all about the encounter in the grange. I told him the details, leaving nothing out about the night. I told him how he had missed a great night, although I did say that if he had been there, it may not have been so frightening with more backup.

"I'd have shit my pants, mate!" he said, laughing so hard that coffee came out of his nose.

Things turned a little more sullen after the laughter died down. Michael took a deep drink of his coffee and swirled the liquid around in the mug before he looked back at me and continued, "I didn't tell you the whole story about cancelling on you, mate."

"It's fine, pal. Honestly, don't worry about it," I said reassuringly.

"I get that, mate. But..." He stopped, looking anxious.

"What's up? You can tell me." I was a little worried now.

He put down his mug and said, "Lucy's sister died last night. She tried to call me to go to the hospital with her, but I was out. She was hit by a car and she died in hospital."

He had not known this girl for too long; he had never even mentioned Lucy had a sister.

"She was only eleven, dude... no fucking age!"

I didn't know what to say to my friend. It was hard to know what to do.

"I'm sorry man, honestly." I tried to console him. "Please send my thoughts to Lucy and her family. They don't know me, and I didn't know—"

"Hannah," Michael interrupted mid-sentence.

I felt sick and my blood ran cold. The girl in the wardrobe was his girlfriend's sister.

I only mentioned briefly to Michael after he had attended the funeral what I saw. It is always difficult when I see things or am visited by spirits without being asked by those left behind. He thanked me and he said that they had found the red box that Hannah had kept her writing in whilst they had been arranging things for her service. Apparently, Hannah was a writer of poetry, and this red box was where she kept her writing. This meant a great deal to the family my friend said. This must have been why I was shown this box. She wanted them to have her writing and remember her that way. I know that he never mentioned what I saw to his girlfriend as she is still to this day traumatised by what happened. I got to know her a little better in the months following Hannah's death, and the only thing I had said to her was that Hannah was at peace. She knew I knew something, and she trusted me. This was enough for her to find a little peace.

4

OUIJA

I didn't have much time over the next few months to go adventuring. I seemed to have a lot on my plate emotionally during that time. I had a lot of negative emotions and depressive thoughts stemming from self-belief and my feeling of being lost. I had my ideas of my spiritual self, but my emotional self and my physical self were becoming darker.

I know that people go through these stages in their lives, and I grew to know this in my life today. However, then I was rebelling against anyone who tried to help me regain my focus. I was not in the best of places with the people I was connected to in any significant way, and my head was spinning out of control. I find at times when feeling quite low, and when we feel lost, there is always a sign to follow, whether this is a belief or a sign from a God, or in the universe opening doors for you. My sign came in the form of a voice in my head. The lady's voice I had heard before was getting stronger, so strong that I felt that this lady had to be my spirit guide. She seemed to be standing out against the negative thoughts I was having, and she seemed to be spurring me on. My mind was not the clearest due to my emotional troubles of the previous few months and so I decided it would be an idea to dabble in the taboo subject of Ouija.

There are so many mixed views about using Ouija boards or spirit boards. They range from rumours that they create doorways to Hell, to myths that they summon demons. Having performed thousands of these sessions throughout my career, both privately and in public events, I find them to be a handy tool to connect to spirit and not some gateway to Hades. Like any method of spirit communication, this must be approached with caution and respect—whether this is using a medium, a pendulum or tarot cards, you must trust yourself and protect yourself however you feel is right. Some people feel saying a prayer is best, or some sit in a circle of light and envision bright light around them. The protection needed is not necessarily from evil forces, but from suggestion, which can lead to people thinking that the spirit is harmful. For example, many times I have been told over a board that I am going to die. *Hmm...* If I let that linger in my head and let that get to me, my mind can create so many worries that I let it rule me, and before you know it, I have let this negative thought manifest into something worse. This is my opinion on how Ouija boards are dangerous, not because the devil lives in it. They are dangerous if mistreated, the same way a Monopoly board is dangerous if you use it wrong. *Those little houses are a choking hazard.* My only advice is use these things carefully and always treat the spirits you encounter with respect, follow the advice of saying goodbye to close down the session, and trust those you play with.

I had acquired an old glass table with chipped silver legs and scratches on the surface of the glass. It had called to me when I was browsing a second-hand shop. *This would be perfect!* I had researched Ouija and had read a lot about the certain practices that should be followed. I drew out the needed features of the board—the alphabet, numbers zero to nine, yes and no, and most importantly – Goodbye. I decorated it with symbols of protection from one of the many books I had acquired. I let the ink dry, collected some candles and let the anticipation swill around in my mind. I felt my mind buzzing. I didn't know exactly what was going to happen, but I was willing to see and excited to find out who I would speak to.

Night-time came around. It was a windy one outside and the rain started to tap on the window heavily, like stones being thrown or the *tap, tap* of skeletal fingers. This sound wouldn't put me off. I was protected in my room in the new house the same way I was in the room at Park Road.

I put a thick cushion down beside the table to get comfortable on. I opted for white candles and had followed a ritual from one of my books to bless the candles for protection. The oil I had used smelt strangely like a Sunday morning when Malc would prep dinner for the family. I placed the candles around the board at each point of the compass—north, south, east and west. I lit the candles in order and then set the white sage burning. *It is time...*

I was nervous and so before I placed my finger on the glass, I took a shot of Jack Daniels, placing my fingers on a tequila shot glass I was using as a planchette. I closed my eyes for a moment, allowing the burning feeling of the bourbon to subside. One deep breath and I started: "I ask any spirit guides and loved ones to come close to me, to protect me and to keep me safe tonight." It was a prayer of mine that I still use today. I pictured an aqua-coloured ball of light surrounding me and spreading out like water consuming the room in beautiful colour. The glass moved. The sound of glass on glass was not a pleasant one, but it eased after a moment, almost gliding over the board rather than scraping. It was as though an energy was between the glass and the table.

I dared not look at first where the glass was moving to, but I convinced myself that I must look. My body was jittering, like the first hit of coffee in the morning. The glass glided to H, and then it continued, becoming more fluent: E-L-L-O.

"Hello?" I said aloud, not really speaking to anyone in particular. My finger on the glass felt cold and it tingled like when you lie on your hand for too long. The glass shot quick enough to startle me. It moved to YES. A shiver ran down my spine, but I was exhilarated.

"Who are you?" I said as I shuffled around, my hand stretched over the glass, candles making the light dance around the room like a smooth waltz.

F – O – R.

"For?" I mimicked like a robot.

Y – O – U.

The glass twisted and twirled around the board smoothly and determined. "You. For you? For me?" The glass glided over to YES.

This was a little scary. Even though I asked, I was now communicating directly to a ghost, and it was claiming that it was here for me.

"What do you want from me?" I asked, eagerly awaiting the glass to pirouette along the board and answer.

G – U – I – D – E – Y – O – U.

"You want to guide me?" I asked. Out loud I must have sounded like a clueless child, but it was all new for me. The glass danced to YES. "Are you the voice I have heard in my head? Are you the lady who I keep hearing?" I was hoping the answer would be yes. I wanted this to be the person who came through. The glass circled smoothly around YES several times as though this was excitement. I heard a sweet little laugh and felt a rush of blood to my cheeks, and I felt myself smile a huge smile in discovering this lady. "Nice to meet you properly, Mrs..." I laughed to myself. It was as though my energy had been taken over by joy and this epiphany of knowledge was giving me a natural high.

Y – V – O – N – N – E. The glass spun around the letters spelling her name.

"Y – von – ee?" I said, having not clicked onto the spelling of her name. The glass spelt the name again and still I didn't click.

I often laugh to myself how this bond with my main spirit guide was created. Even to this day, I laugh and am reminded of how daft it was I couldn't pronounce her name. Once I caught on, I greeted her properly. "It is a pleasure to meet you properly, Yvonne."

But I wanted more. I needed to know why me and who she was. I asked her exactly that. "Why me, Yvonne? How do you know me?"

The glass spun its web of letters. Yvonne spelt out that she knew me in a past life. She was a midwife who helped to deliver my child in a past life. She spoke of how I had died and where I had lived. She said that I was shot outside a church and that I had died of infection in the nineteen-forties. I asked for the dates and the location because I wanted to see if there were any records. I was shocked to see that there was a record of the incident and everything fit. This gave me the reason I had to trust this spirit.

Yvonne gave me a lot of advice about things I had been thinking about. She gave me guidance that I had really needed at that moment in time, and she left the session by spinning the glass to spell: I – A – M – H – E – R – E. I felt comfort and reassurance by having this lady to guide me. I felt that we matched pretty well. She was quite the dirty-humoured lady who spoke as it is, not mincing words and sometimes using language so vulgar that it would make people blush. But she was my guide! Nowadays I call her Ronnie, or Ron, because she still jokes about the name confusion that first time. She helps me with my readings today and has helped me through a lot of scary times.

During the whole session, the room was not cold, there was nothing unpleasant, and there was a peaceful calm over the whole of the environment. The devil never came for my soul and there was no exorcism required afterwards. All was well. Do not be fooled by this positive experience, however. Sometimes, taking a spirit board to a negative or more haunted location, it doesn't always have that same feeling to it. Sometimes this can result in there being a lot more to the story then a spirit guide wanting to come through to say hi.

5

THE ASYLUM ON THE HILL

Life was not always calm for me growing up. I was finding juggling my paranormal life and my regular life difficult because only a handful of people were interested in the paranormal and spirituality. My family was moving on with a much more peaceful existence now we had moved away from the terrors of the old family home, so I did not want to really involve them in more of the spooky world I was living in. I found that I had to bury my interest and my abilities sometimes and practice alone. I longed for and searched for more like-minded people who could teach me more. This search would take a long time, years in fact, before I felt comfortable again to open up fully and embrace my own weirdness. In the meantime, I continued to venture out, to connect more with Ronnie and to walk the woods and the local area alone.

Sometimes when you spend so much time holding inside the real you, it can cause some pretty severe mental health issues, and my journey was no different. I was in an unhealthy relationship. I had shut away people who had joked about my gifts, and I had been beaten down to a shell of what I felt was me. This all changed one day when I decided to free myself of these restraints and said to myself, "No more!" I broke away from the unhealthy relationships after some time and started opening up again. The walks and the areas I investigated myself were becoming more intense, as I was once again freeing my own spirit and embracing the feelings and the connections to the spirit world.

I sat one night thinking a lot about life and heard Ronnie speak to me so clearly, saying she was proud I was free. I decided I wanted to celebrate, and what better way to celebrate than some spooky fun? I had heard of an abandoned hospital and asylum that was boarded up but you could still gain access if you were daring enough to sneak through a window. This seemed a hell of a place to go to, so this was my plan. Finding the place was difficult. Anyone I had spoken to had greeted me with the same answer of, "Should you really be doing that?" or "You don't want to go messing in places like that. They're dangerous!" *That is why it is fun,* were my thoughts when greeted by these diversions. I wasn't a kid; I was around twenty-four and mature... Well, I was twenty-four.

Finally, I had come across the details of where this place was located and so I packed up my bag and decided to go it alone. Torch, batteries and warm clothes, and I was set! I managed to get a bus to the main street of the village and then followed the directions to a small layby by the woods. My mind was racing, and I was admittedly nervous due to the weather being rainy and cold—typical British summertime. It was not an easy place to find. It was like the land this building was on had been taken back by nature. Some unholy force had allowed the woods and the stinging nettles to grow fiercely around, keeping in whatever evil was there.

I was in the layby under the shadow of trees that seemed to lean away from the building located in the middle of everything. It was like the trees were afraid to look at what was in the clearing. I remember setting my first foot into the woods and the wind blew through the trees and the sound of cracking twigs underfoot sounded like I was treading on bones of the past. *Snap!* With each step, I was treading on the dead and suffering of this land and the woods grew darker. I felt excited but sick at the same time. No one knew where I was going because I wanted to avoid being treated like a child, and I didn't want to be stopped. Each step felt wrong. I was being pushed forward by my longing for adventure and being pulled backwards by the thought of the pain and suffering I could sense in this place even though I had not been inside.

"Shhh." A voice came from behind me. I stopped and my eyes crept to look behind me while my head dared not move. I could see a shape in the trees, and I forced my head to turn to see. It faded as my eyes focused, but I could have sworn I had seen a hooded figure. My pace was speeding up, the rain was falling harder through the trees bringing a shiver to my body. "Hey!" a gruff, angry voice said again— closer this time! I turned around to catch the perpetrator and was shocked to see the hooded figure standing, peering out from behind a tree. I lost my footing but caught my balance by reaching for a tree. The shape disappeared into the haze of the trees with a sort of *pop*. The air seemed to buzz and mould around the sound, and the rain that had fallen on those trees shook down in a small but deliberate cascade.

This was the point I nearly turned back, but I asked Ronnie to keep me safe. Ronnie and I had formed a fun friendship in my time with her. She was (and still is to this day) a foul-mouthed and sarcastic pain in my arse; but I do love her and she keeps me safe. I could see a slick side smile in my mind, seeing her wrinkles on her cheeks, and I felt safe.

"You're not going to stop me!" I shouted out, not knowing if this was a living person, some spirit trying to scare me, or even a trick of my mind, but I seemed to get my courage back. I set off again, heading up the sloping woodlands. The rain was beating down in droves and I wanted to be inside. The trees seemed to be getting older as I got nearer to the top of the woods. The branches creaked like moans of the elderly, cracking in the wind as though the sheer weight of their leaves was a strain. The branches were getting bare too, the closer I got, and the air seemed thinner. I remember my chest started to tighten and I felt pressure starting to hammer down until my legs ached and my mind was clouded. Doubt in my mind started to question whether I was ever going to find this place or would I be lost in the woods?

The trees opened up and there it was—a brick fortress surrounded by stinging nettles and vines canvasing the building like a curse of some wicked witch. The walls were stained with moss and age, and the windows were boarded with silver metal plates. Here and there was tagged with graffiti and urban art. Pictures of lobotomies and screaming faces painted with such details shook my body with the thoughts these pictures provoked. The wind whistled through the space between me and the building, spirits within tempting me to take my chances and see if I made it out alive. I walked past a fire escape and the door atop was gone, replaced by a solid steel plate. Around the back of the building, I felt strange. The energy of this place seemed lonely, and it made me feel sad and confused. I noticed no animals, no birds flying overhead, and I thought, *Not even the animals want to be here*. Gravel was underfoot and it scratched at the bottom of my Converse shoes. Stones flicked as I trod and occasionally they would hit the building. The rain had slowed but the clouds above me were angry. They threatened thunder, I was certain.

I stood looking up at the boarded-up windows and took it all in. This place was huge. I had been walking for around ten minutes and had not done a full perimeter of the building. Something hit me then—a stone on the side of my head. It came sharply and fell to the ground. My head turned to the direction from which it came but there was no one there. My own footsteps seemed to be getting louder as I walked on. The sounds I was hearing seemed to echo strongly inside my head. I felt something stalking me, even though I couldn't see it. It felt as though this stalker was following me to scare me off. It felt similar to the presence I felt in the woods earlier, so I was fully aware this was not someone living, messing around with me. I wasn't being frightened off, though. This place was teeming with energy, and I needed to get my fix.

As I rounded the side of the building, I passed by another fire escape. This time there was a window at the top of the black cold stairway that was open. The metal plate had been removed. This was my entrance point! I climbed over a gate to the fire escape and slipped, grazing my leg on the hard metal. There was sticky black paint all over the metal that clung to my clothes and my hands. It was not everywhere, though. This seemed to be a lazy attempt to keep people out when the place was closed. The stairs rang out like bells as I took each step. The hollow ringing was like a countdown to me reaching the window. As I got to the top, I looked behind and felt the presence of the stalker once more. I heard a cough, strong and dry, and heard something light hit the gate below, which took me by surprise, so I took the last few steps two at a time and vaulted in through the window. I was inside.

The hallway I was in smelt damp and dusty. The floors were littered with tiles and broken doors. There were papers thrown all over the ground, and the light from outside had found ways to shine through the cracks and small holes in the blocked-up windows. It gave an odd feeling looking down the long hallway with scattered light bleeding through. There were warnings of asbestos on the walls, so I used my shirt as a makeshift mask to keep me safer. The corridor had rooms on both sides, and I explored each room. The first one I entered looked like a private room. There was the skeletal remains of a single bed and a small wardrobe. The room made me feel claustrophobic, and I felt the sudden racing of my heart. I ran out, my foot sliding on a tile as I slipped through the doorway. I scrambled through and laughed to myself.

I noticed laughter from somewhere around me. It echoed and hit off the walls and my skin bumped up in reaction to this sound. I looked both ways and saw nothing, but this laugh was close. *Don't be scared off!* I thought to myself. The other rooms were very similar to the first one—all painted white and all littered with the remains of beds and broken wardrobes. One room housed a handmade noose hanging from the wardrobe. (Although, I do feel that this was something added by someone for fright and not something that had been used.) I got no weird vibes from this. I felt this was likely something a squatter or someone trying to scare people had created.

I made a conscious effort to remember my way back. It felt that this place would easily be somewhere one could get lost. I got a pen out of my backpack and wrote down which ways I had turned and made sure I could follow the directions back again.

I reached a broken glass-panelled door and squeezed through. On the wall sprayed in red paint was "WELCOME TO HELL!" *Nice!* The stairs went darker the farther I went, and I decided to try to explore as much as I could, so I exited the stairwell on the next floor. Another broken door hanging off its hinges made way to a larger room. This looked like a recreational room and the space made me feel worse. The floor was littered still with rubbish and broken parts of the building, but the room seemed busy. I stood perfectly still but could hear things moving. I could hear voices, but these reverberated around me and through me. It felt thick with energy. My torch started to flicker, and I hit it on my leg to get it to start up again. It always seemed to help. They always say hit something and it'll fix it—I found this with most things. The voices seemed to settle down as I asked Ronnie to quiet them down again. My hand went cold, as though it had put it in ice. I closed my eyes and the icy feeling turned into a small delicate grip. I felt fingers close around my hand, and this feeling of loss came to me and made tears well up in my eyes. I opened them again and looked down and momentarily saw a shadow fall away from my hand. I shook myself and refocussed.

There was a dividing wall between the rec room and another big room that had a large hole in it. The walls were sprayed with some very impressive artwork that had been sprayed by urban explorers, and I couldn't help admiring that. This room felt colder and I could feel something that was not like the echoed recordings on the building. I felt I was being watched and that it was a strong presence. I looked around, shining my torch around the walls and the broken tables but could see nothing. There was a doorway farther toward the corner of the room that had a darker sense to it. The light looked murky and there was a sinister feeling that something had happened there. There was clattering coming from this room. Tiles were being kicked and tossed around in warning.

"Hello?" I shouted out. *There could be someone else here... Be careful!* I told myself. There was a shadow in the light as though whoever or whatever was causing the sounds was standing close. "Is there anyone there?" The shaking in my voice was making my anxiety noticeable. The shape came out a foot or two before dissolving into thin air. There was a strange sound as this happened, another *pop* that made the room feel fuzzy and strange. My head felt as though I had taken a shot of whiskey. I was so curious about this shadow and this sound, so I decided to follow the source and go through the murky doorway. This led to another corridor just like the others, with litter and busted broken ceiling tiles so thick you couldn't see the floor. There was a door to the left that led to more stairs, but it was the far end of the corridor I was drawn to. I heard my guide in my head telling me it was probably not the best idea to go down there. I was taken back in my mind to Park Road where the walls seemed to breathe and the world spun. I remembered the feeling of knowing something was not right and that at any moment, George, from back in that house, was out to get me. I shook off this memory and took my first step forward into this new corridor and toward this darkened room where no light could reach.

As I passed the door on the left of the stairs there was no light there either. The farther you went into the bowels of this place, the less light there was. I passed it quickly, not wanting to be drawn there when I needed to see what was in this far room. The closer I got, the thicker the air. It was as though the floor was grabbing at my shoes–trapped souls reaching up trying to save me. I struggled through the mess and made it to the doorway. It was another small space, an office of sorts with a cupboard to the back right of the room. My torchlight lit the room up and shone on the stained walls.

As I stepped inside, I felt a sudden rush of hot air. It was like the devil breathing on my face. The heat reached my lips through the shirt that covered my face, and it took me aback. I reached out and regained my balance, standing strong. I looked around for a source of this but found only a broken desk and an open cupboard. The cupboard door was swinging. I walked in and tried to close it, but it wouldn't budge. There was nothing blocking the door and this seemed to be a warning sign to my brain at the time. I backed off and walked to the desk. There was a littering of papers that had yellowed with time and damp had stuck them together. I was startled by a coughing sound coming from the door I had come through. My torch immediately shot to the cause of the sound but there was no one there. This was amazing! I remember my smile growing on my face. I was shaking with fear, but I felt so alive.

I can imagine how people may see my actions and may question my sanity, but I can assure you that I felt safe enough with my guides protecting me. But, well, yeah, maybe I could be a little loopy.

I started to feel quite sick in this room. There was a lump in the back of my throat and I felt I could have been sick. I walked back around the desk. The door to the cupboard creaked as I passed it, and I felt something pull on the shirt I had wrapped around my neck. I shouted out in shock as I fought to take it back. As suddenly as it had caught, my shirt released. I ran to the door with the shirt in my hand. I looked back and saw a flash of a shadow, but it was so quick that I was unsure what I had seen. How things can change in a few seconds.

I stepped out of the room and walked back towards the staircase to the lower levels. These stairs were dark and littered with broken glass. I stood atop the stairs and met the front doors to the building. There were doors on either side of the large doorway and light flickered in from outside. There was a broken bare bed in the middle of the open space and yet more litter. I walked down the stairs and took a glance around through the doors. To the right of the main door, there was a smell from the corridor. It was dank and it was putrid. It was the kind of smell you get from open sewer works. It was the most nauseous I had ever felt while looking down that dark hallway. I stepped back but the smell followed me. My whole body shivered with this hot flush. My face felt hot like someone had put their hands on my cheeks. I was walking backwards, still looking at the dark passageway. I hadn't looked behind me towards the left of the doorway, so I had no idea what I was stepping back into.

I could see a shape coming from the dark in front of me. It was moving in slow motion and it looked solid. I didn't speak. I just saw this shadow vibrating quickly as it moved. It was wearing a broad-brimmed hat and it stood out against the blackness of the dark that embraced it. I fell backwards for what seemed like an eternity. My foot had slipped on a wet tile. I felt as though I was falling to Hell. As I struck the floor, I felt the wind knocked out of me on impact.

The worst part of this came when I was trying to catch my breath. There were hands on my shoulders—cold, bony hands pulling at my clothes as I lay on my back, unable to breathe. The fear was real and I was aware of this feeling of something coming out of the dark in front of me—something more than just spirit, something older. It felt more demonic. I have rarely felt this feeling since, but it is a real fear that I would not want anyone else to feel.

The smell had gotten worse, and as I regained my breath and clawed my way to my feet, I ran. I ran up the stairs, my shoes sliding on the broken glass, sending me to my knees. I felt the glass slice through my jeans and the warm oozing of blood trickling down and through the denim. It didn't hurt at the time. I was focused solely on the light shining through the broken doors at the top of the stairwell. I reached the top and fell through the door, breathless, with my leg beginning to ache. I turned around to see the form of a man standing on the landing wearing the broad-brimmed hat.

I didn't see his face because his head was lowered. His coat was worn and threadbare in places. He was covered in dust and grime that gave him a homeless look. His hat was black, but the material looked almost alive. The colour seemed to suck in any light. I felt dizzy as my eyes began to get lost in the depths. I could feel my head start to turn with a hypnotic effect. My eyes pulsed and my head swam in a haze. I felt as though I was being absorbed by this thing.

The form under the hat didn't move forward, and it didn't make sounds as my feet had when treading on the broken glass. It simply vibrated and looked as though it had been paused on an old VHS, jittering as if it was made of static. The hat, though... The hat held more power, I felt. My blood felt hot. I could feel burning behind my eyes like staring at the TV too long. My heartbeat started to slow down as though it were going to stop. This was nothing I had felt before. There was hot air rising from this thing and I felt breathing behind my neck, like a kiss of a demonic force.

Suddenly a sound of smashing tiles came from behind me. It shook me and my gaze was snapped away from this entity in front of me. I immediately glanced back again and there was nothing in front of me. I took it upon myself to run. My knee was throbbing, and I felt blood running down into my shoe. I bashed myself through the glass doors and into the corridor where I had experienced the shirt pull, and while running, I glanced back and was greeted by the figure in the hat. I didn't stop to get lost in its energy this time. I ran faster and into the rec room. There were two people in there now, real people, living people, and I ran headlong into them and we fell to the floor in a crash.

The two guys in their early twenties grumbled and complained as we rolled out of the huddle. "What the hell you doing, man?!" the taller of the two shouted while brushing off his jacket and sitting up. "Where's the fire, bro?" He spoke in a Birmingham accent and searched around on his floor for his glasses.

"Seriously, man!" said the shorter of the two. "You made me shit my pants!" he joked and stood up, offering me a hand.

My chest was burning from the run and my eyes were seeing

After Park Road

stars as the blood rushed to my head. I looked back in the direction of the stairway and panted.

"Sorry, guys..." I started between gasps of oxygen. "There was some... thing chasing me, and I didn't see you." I must have sounded crazy as the pair laughed.

"You seen a ghost, bro?" the taller one laughed and walked past me to look down the corridor. "Nothing there now, mate." He walked back, looking confident he was braver than I was.

A small rock was thrown at him from the corridor, and he ran back to where the shorter man and I stood. None of us looked brave now, and he most certainly sped back quicker than he wanted us to notice.

Nothing else was thrown once we were all huddled close together, and the atmosphere seemed to lift a little. I began to allow myself to relax some. I asked if they had made the breaking noises moments ago and they admitted it was them. They had been shifting things around to do some more artwork on the walls and had felt the urge to be destructive. I introduced myself, and they did the same. Colin was the tough-looking tall guy, and the shorter, stout one was Bruce.

Once I was more relaxed, I made a joke that they were like the Mario Brothers. They had heard this a few times apparently but shared in my humour. I told them about what I had seen and they actually took me seriously, which I did not expect. This had been their second time sneaking in, and they had heard and seen things, but never this man with the hat. Bruce worked as a paramedic and offered to take a look at my leg. He was more prepared than I was, bringing with him a first aid kit.

We sat chatting in the more positive atmosphere and shared a drink from a flask I had brought along with me. They told me about hearing crying from some of the rooms and seeing smoke from a hallway down the stairs I had run from.

Thunder started to break outside making us all jump. "I think we best call it a day, buddy," Colin said to his friend, half-asking and half-telling him it was the good idea.

Bruce nodded and started to get his stuff together. They both had turned on their head torches a bit earlier, as the darkness of the storm brewing outside made the room fill with shadows. I limped up, my leg hurting more and more, and headed for the hole in the wall and the stairway back to the top floor and the window I came through.

The energy became uneasy as we left this room, and none of us wanted to be last in our three-man conga line. Another stone was thrown—it missed us. Then another stone, and another stone and another. Soon this became like a barrage of stones, each the size of a pebble but each hit close to us like the spirits were chasing us out. We all freaked out, as this stone throwing was getting more aggressive. The guys ran a good few steps ahead of me and they reached the staircase a good thirty seconds before I did. I think I did well with a cut leg and was glad that, as we climbed the stairs, the stones simply fell down the stairwell and away from sight.

Colin and Bruce helped me up the last few steps and held me up because my leg was weak. Now on the top floor, we all felt that little bit safer. Colin jumped as a raindrop dripped on his face from a leak in the roof. Bruce laughed and I joined in laughing at his own fear. It is funny that when you get scared in situations like this, laughter is something infectious and it is something that grows the more fearful you are. I started humming *Singing in the Rain* to Bruce's amusement. I was in front by this time, walking with Colin's help down the narrow corridor to the exit.

"Stop laughing, you little shit!" Colin said with the annoyance ripe in his voice. We turned around and saw that Bruce looked white.

"That isn't me, mate," Bruce said with a shaky voice.

The sound of laughter sounded like something from a *Scooby Doo* episode, and it resonated around the corridor. None of us were keen to investigate, and we hurried to reach our escape. They helped me out the window at the speed of light, nearly throwing me out before they both leapt out into the rain together. I hopped a few steps at a time and reached the gate where the two helped me over. Our hands were covered in the black anti-vandalism paint and slipped on the wet metal rails. Colin was the last one over the gate, and as he landed on the muddy ground, Bruce made a strange squeaking sound and pointed to the window. Standing there was the man in the hat, his face shadowed by its wide brim. We all stood still, me leaning on Bruce's shoulder. That familiar ringing feeling started, and my eyes began to pulse in their sockets. I grabbed and slapped Bruce on the shoulder and he shook his head, grabbing Colin's shoulder and pulling him to make him snap out of it.

"LET'S GO!" Bruce shouted and they half-carried and half-dragged me as we made our way away from the window around the front of the building and towards the edge of the woods.

We came to rest on a broken-down wall by the side of what remained of the driveway to the hospital. The storm clouds in the sky above the decrepit building looked beautiful. The sun was out brightly behind us and the contrast between dark and light was incredible. We were soaked and our clothes were filthy. My shoes and my coat were stained but I was thankful to be out of there.

"Do you do this often, Andy?" Colin asked me.

"Only when I have something to celebrate, mate." I laughed heartily.

"Well..." Bruce said, "you're a brave man going in there on your own." He was looking down at a tear in his jeans. "I think that's it for our decorating here, Col, if that's all right with you."

Colin smiled and nodded.

We steadily walked back through the woods. The green light shining through the trees on our way back through seemed so much friendlier than on my way up. We all slipped a little through the wet undergrowth, but it was fun, and we all laughed at one another. We arrived back at the layby and Colin got out his keys for his green Citroen Saxo that was parked out front. He gave me a lift home and as we parted, we shook hands and said our goodbyes.

"Don't take this wrong, mate, but I hope we don't see you again.

We haven't had a fright like that before. I think you're a bad omen... A nice guy but a bad omen!"

We all laughed, and I exited the car and went inside the house. They seemed to be genuinely nice people, and I do regret that I never kept in contact with them.

Strange as it may seem to some, including me, I did venture back to the asylum years later before it was knocked down. A few members of a ghost hunting group and I were out on a road trip and the guy driving had heard of somewhere he wanted to check out and drove us to the same layby. We pulled up and I shivered. I didn't want to get out of the car. I had never told anyone about my experience in this place because, honestly, it was a darker place that I like to experience. But we ventured through the woods and up to the mammoth of a building. We used the exact same staircase I had used to get into the window previously. I avoided getting my Converses ruined this time, though. We went as far as the recreational rooms before we heard the same sound as I had before—hammering of tiles and breaking of glass. Those who accompanied me were worried because they didn't know what was down that darkened hallway. We left after only being in the building for about twenty minutes. I was glad that we had not seen the same figure I had seen the first time. I felt glad when I had heard they had knocked the place down because whatever I had felt that time, I felt it needed to stay buried.

One of the most common questions I get in my capacity as a ghost hunter is, "Are you afraid that spirit will follow you home?" My answer here is normally no. I don't feel that spirits ever want to follow people home. Why would they? I find that spirits linger and haunt places that mean a lot to them or places where they felt at home. They also follow people and guide those they loved or cared for in life. Spirit guides or guardian angels tend to guide those they have a connection to, whether in this life or another. So, no, I normally say.

However, in the case of the man in the hat, I did see him again. I have seen him twice outside of the asylum. The first time was about a week later while I was walking home from work. I saw him at the end of the old railway line near the town centre of Coalville. I had walked through the shortcut on my way home, and he was standing there watching me. I had the same feeling of dread and fear that I had felt in the asylum, but without the hypnotic effect. I stood watching him, and he faded away into the dark of the night.

The second time was about a month later, and he stood by the clock tower as I was on my way to the pub. He stood completely alone. My body still shivers today as it shivered that last time clear as day. I looked across the road to the pub I was on my way to, and he had moved to the crossing in a matter of a second. I ran across the road and nearly got hit by a car, but luckily I got into the pub without incident. That was the last time I saw him. It didn't have the same effect on me because I believe its power was linked to the building where I first saw it. I don't know much about that hospital or its history, but I do feel that when it closed, darker things took over the halls and dark corners before the building was demolished.

6

CRIES IN THE RIVER

Since my experience at the asylum and seeing this being in my everyday life, I did feel that my development and my spiritual side were getting out of control, and I was afraid I was doing something wrong or maybe that the universe was trying to tell me I needed to slow it down. I was thrilled how strong I had experienced these things and how much I had seen, but the thought of me attracting the nasty things in the paranormal scared me at the time... perhaps I was thinking too much or maybe it was too much mental trash clogging up my head that was making me feel out of control. I had been through a lot in my personal life, and I did feel I had to take some time for me. I swapped the paranormal adventures for a soul-searching adventure and went off backpacking around Europe. I was gone for around six months and it was the perfect time to clear my head and also to realise that I was sure my path was certain in the paranormal. While I was away, I was still drawn to Spirit and the paranormal found me in the places that I went—such as the Coliseum in Rome and in a small bar in Dublin—some of the most memorable of encounters. The fact I was found when in my paranormal break was a sure sign it was meant to be. When I returned to the UK, I reconnected with a spiritual development group. We had agreed to go out on our own little investigation. We were all spiritually open and eager to go on more adventures. These people were my people. They loved the stories and the adventures I had told them about.

Hesitantly, they asked if we could visit the ruins I had visited alone so long ago. I agreed and we set about packing some paranormal equipment and headed for a drink before we would go into the woods. We packed CB radios so that we could split up into the woods and around the ruins and still be in contact. The good thing about these radios is that being in the middle of nowhere, we would get no interference. We packed K2 meters and we packed our dowsing rods and our crystal pendulums. We all, of course, had our spiritual and mediumistic qualities too. After our drink, Jo, Kelly Brian and I headed into the woods.

The sky was clear and the stars were out in force. It felt safer having us all together, and it didn't feel nearly as foreboding. We went along the mud path towards the tunnel bridge. We stopped and I led us through and explained what I had picked up on before. We joined hands under the bridge and I spoke out, "If there is any spirit here that wishes to communicate, then make yourself known to us." My voice seemed to encircle us and bounce around the tunnel. The tone went sombre, and Kelly gripped my hand tightly and moved closer to me.

She whispered, "It feels like there is someone behind me."

I opened my eyes and glanced behind her. A cold breeze came across my cheek and I saw flashes in my vision. I encouraged her to ask spirit to do something. She was afraid and refused. In situations like this, I do like to test whether spirit can push their boundaries.

I took it upon myself to call out again, "If that was spirit behind my friend, then do something more... Touch her or make a sound."

My voice rung out but silence ensued. We all waited for a sign. A knocking sound became apparent and filled the tunnel with deliberate knocks in repetitions of two—once, twice and three more times.

Kelly clambered in closer to me and Brian. This is what we wanted and since I was not alone in this situation, I was unafraid.

We dropped hands and we got out our equipment. The K2 meter was not moving, but all of our dowsing rods pointed the same ways as we asked where this spirit was located. We identified a man who had died in the road nearby. He was not malicious, but he was drunk at the time, so as I connected to his energy, it felt as though he was still having to come to terms with this guilt he felt. Brian felt the presence of a dog with the man, and he concluded that he felt the man he called David used to walk his dog down this way. This all seemed to validate the things I had seen before. The man who was grumpy with the dog beside him. This was an amazing night, as I had forgotten to mention to my friends about the dog walker.

Getting through the tunnel bridge, things felt fine and relaxed. The sky was beautiful and the woods were calm. We walked under the waterway that I had climbed up before and felt nothing. *How is this so different?* I quizzed myself, and I wondered if the energies that had lay here before had found peace.

Once the path started to become overgrown, though, things started to change. There were trees hanging over the path and Brian stopped suddenly as a *thud* ahead made him back off. I was following at the back of the pack but hurried to the front as he stopped with a yelp.

"What's up Brian? What did you see?" I said excitedly, annoyed I had missed something.

"A figure dropped from the tree in front of us!" He was almost hysterical, which I found funny. He was pointing his torch ahead. "It couldn't have been an animal. It was wearing a helmet or something!"

"I believe you, mate, don't worry." This was different to when I was here previously. "You want to swap places and you go to the back?" I offered.

Brian nodded and went to the back of the line with Kelly. I noticed they held hands for comfort. I found myself stopping by the fork-off point where I felt the presence of a monk. I remembered the feeling of this energy before and I shuddered. I stopped and asked Jo for the K2 meter and she fetched it out, pressing the grey button to turn it on. The meter's five lights sparked into life and flashed up from green to amber and then red. A K2 meter picks up on the electromagnetic field that spirit theoretically affect. There was no electricity out in the woods and our radios were switched off so there was nothing we had on us that could cause this. The lights went to red and continued to flicker at the red light, showing there was a strong electromagnetic field.

Jo spoke up. "Can you step back from the machine please?" Straight away the lights went to green.

This is amazing!! I thought, stepping from foot to foot to keep warm in the sudden cold air.

"If this is the spirit of a holy man, please can you come close again and make the lights go red?" Jo was feeling empowered. It was clear in her voice she was loving this. She was always a bit of a tech girl. The lights rose to red and they stayed there. The meter made its low, level ticking sound like a hummingbird. Jo was somewhat of a skeptic; she believed in Spirit and she had given a few spiritual messages to us all before, but she was not as convinced as the rest of us. The levels on the meter went down again and we all looked up the pathway into the dark as a snapping sound drew our attention.

"You've chased him away, Jo!" I laughed, and the rest of the group joined in. "Go get him." I said, pointing up the darker path.

Without warning, Jo called my bluff and walked alone up the path, whistling loudly. She got to where the path started to turn and stood still, looking back at us.

"I don't think he likes strong women, guys!" she shouted back whilst doing a silly jig. We took some pictures while she was standing there and got a few orbs on the pictures, but in the woods these could have been insects or anything that wasn't paranormal.

On her way back from the edge of the path, she turned suddenly and let out a gasp. She had felt something graze her back and her side and she seemed to speed up to get to us.

"Something got me!" she said, lifting up her top at the back. She had four scratches deep enough to draw blood. This sent cold runs down my spine. The scratches looked like nail marks and they were fresh. Her top had not been damaged, and it is hard to believe her excuse that it must have been a twig from the bushes. I could see in her face that she didn't want to admit the more likely cause of these abrasions. Out of all the investigations I have been on to date, this was the most convinced I have ever been where I believe a physical wound has been caused by something spiritual.

The others were more concerned than Jo, and Brian and Kelly did question whether we should turn back. Gladly we did not because the night was getting interesting.

We reached the gate where I had seen the figures that sank into the ground. The field was lit up by the stars and the occasional headlight that passed by the road around the grounds. I was apprehensive, but I suggested we go for a walk through there and skip over the steppingstones in the stream to reach the ruins. The group agreed, and we took it in turns to get over the gate and into the field. The field felt strange underfoot, like the grass and the earth were actually sinking. There was a strange sound like a motor running and it faded then grew louder. We all heard it as we all tried to find the source with our torches. Nothing was there—no electrics and no machinery. It was just us.

The sound changed the closer to the middle of the field we got. There were rocks in the middle that we made our base. We sat down and each poured ourselves a drink. While we were talking, Kelly pointed towards the ruins over the stream. There was a smoky figure. She was far away, but we all saw this shape walking along the edge of the field by the ruins.

Brian called out loudly, "HELLO!"

We all stood, anticipating what was going to be this thing's response. I was taken back to the scene in *Ghostbusters* when they shouted, "Get her!" in the library, only to have the ghost launch a scream at them. Thankfully this did not happen, and the shape went

After Park Road

behind one of the structures and did not emerge on the other side. This image was also not captured on any of the pictures we had taken.

I asked if we were ready to go have a look, but only Jo was willing to have a look with me. We left our things with the others and went to the edge of the stream. Turning on our radios, we did a check, and all was good. We crossed carefully and slowly to avoid a cold dip in the water, and we successfully reached the other side. We walked silently to the remains where we had seen the snowy form but there was no sign; however, I could smell something in the air, sage or something earthy and burnt. It was thick and it made my nose itch. Jo radioed over to the others across the stream to ask them if they could see anything. There was no answer. I was searching everywhere around the ruins for any sign of a fire or any sign of anyone who had had a similar idea to us, but we were all alone. Jo was waving her torch over to the others across the stream. We could see them over there with their torches on, but they were not hearing us on the radios.

Jo shouted loudly, "Turn your bloody radio on!"

A few seconds passed and Brian responded, "It is bloody on!"

She complained to me about how they were mistreating her equipment but laughed it off.

We walked around the ruins and experienced a sullen feeling. Jo kept asking me if I felt it, and I did. She kept saying she felt sick, and we actually had to stop at a couple of places because she was getting stomach pains. This was not like her; I had never known her to fake anything, and she admitted that she had never felt this weird or this kind of thing before. I radioed over to the others to come over and help because Jo was being affected badly. The radio answered with loud static and a whistle. This was starting to feel a little how I had felt before—teased by something awful.

The radio went off again and a mumbled voice came over the radio and spoke in what sounded like French. It was not clear, and so when it stopped, I tried again. "Guys! You need to get over here!" I was starting to worry about my friend because she looked very pale and ill, and I was on my own with her. "GUYS!" I snapped over the radio, and the French-sounding voice crackled into action again.

Jo cursed some obscenities and tried to stand up straight. We walked a little farther and reached the large chimney structure at the edge of the ruins. I heard the radio static again, but this time Kelly's voice perked up. "Andy... We need help here. There is this shadow standing by the steppingstones and we can't get across."

Jo was shaken, it was clear to see. We heard them shouting but it was inaudible. Brian was shouting loudly as though his "fierce" voice was going to scare this thing away.

"Come on, Jo. Let's move on if you can." I tried to take my friend's weight to help her along, but she was clearly not well. "We're on our way." I was annoyed because I realised we shouldn't have split up, but that's hindsight. Without warning, the radios blared to life again and babies were screaming through the speakers. Loud and unhappy cries so loud through all of our radios, we could hear them from our friend's radios as we got closer to the water. The volume on the radios went in waves of louder to quiet and loud again. This chilled us all, and we wondered where this could possibly come from. Jo had almost forgotten her pain as we picked up the pace towards the stream and the steppingstones. There was no shadow that we could see, but we did see the form of our friends in an embrace, holding each other close through fear. We met one another's stares even through the dark, and the cries cut off from all the radios as the batteries died.

We stood and looked all around. Torches like searchlights sought out anyone in danger. We searched around, shining our torches in the stream, but the slow-moving water just trickled by calmly. I felt sick and I felt overwhelmed. There was a heavy emotional feeling over everyone in this place now. Jo was able to stand up and the pain had gone as quickly as it had first started.

We headed over the stones and back to the others. They had experienced a shadow standing at the edge of the water, crouching down with their hands in the water. It had disappeared as our torches came closer. I trusted these people; I knew they were honest and wouldn't have done anything to scare us without telling us they had afterwards.

Jo was shaking. She sat on one of the rocks at our base, shaking her head. She sipped on some sweet tea that we gave her to calm her down. "It felt as though my insides were being ripped out," she said, not truly believing what she was saying. "And then... and then those cries..." She held back tears. "I don't want to know what happened here, Andy."

Brian and Kelly were silent during all of this. They were not sure what to say, and I do feel that they felt a sorrow similar to mine for what Jo felt and sensed that night.

There was shouting from a distance that woke us all from our thoughtfulness, and we decided that enough was enough. The shouting sounded as though it was some kind of re-enactment from an epic battle, but it had no source. We couldn't understand the words being shouted; we heard only the shouts from a distance, but it was enough. We didn't agree on conclusions from what we thought the source of the shouting was. Brian said it was someone "pulling our chains," and Kelly and Jo didn't share any thoughts. Kelly was too scared, I think, and she just wanted to get back to the cars.

We hurried through the woods quite silently. The fact we were drained and in quite low moods I think made it hard for any spirits on the way back through the woods to use our energy to make anything happen. Or maybe, it was because we were all too distracted and despondent to notice even if there was any activity.

We got to the cars and we drove home. I only saw Kelly occasionally at our development group. Brian changed jobs about a year later and gave up on ghost hunting, and Jo actually settled down and moved away. We spoke often of the crying from the radios, and none of us could rationalise or debunk that as anything other than paranormal. Jo came to the ruins sceptical but left knowing that there was tragedy in this place that left a scar on the earth and on her own memory.

These were but a few of the adventures on my own and with friends. It has been scary at times, and as I found out that time I went to the ruins with my friends, Spirit pick on people differently and we as people will interpret spiritual energy differently. Jo was very susceptible to the energies around the ruins, and I feel that they showed her some tragic experiences they had.

These stories may sound scary and make people wonder why I would dedicate my life to this work and this amount of unknown and possible dangers. My children today ask me, "Why do you talk to ghosts? Aren't you scared?"

My answer to them is, "Yes, I am scared. But I am also in awe that spirits choose me to bring through messages and guidance. Spirits, for the most part, want to tell their story; they don't want to have their stories and lives forgotten." I tell my eldest daughter, "It is like I am telling their stories and leaving lasting words for people to read and interpret in their own way." But no matter the fears I have felt and the injuries I have had in my pursuit of the paranormal, the good outweighs the bad, and I would never change my life if I could.

I will continue to work with Spirit and the paranormal for as long as I can. I will keep sharing my stories and the stories of the spirits I encounter. I will always embrace this gift I have been given and then when the time comes for me to join the spirit world, who knows? Maybe someone like me will tell my story.

OTHER BOOKS BY ANDREW HOPKINS

The Haunting On Park Road

Printed in Great Britain
by Amazon